Cassowaries

Victoria Blakemore

Copyright info/picture credits

Cover, kohy/AdobeStock; Page 3, Andrea Izzotti/AdobeStock; Page 5, mattiaath/AdobeStock; Page 7, bernswaelz/Pixabay; Page 9, quickshooting/AdobeStock; Pages 10-11, Pomaikai/AdobeStock; Page 13, RalfBeck/Pixabay; Page 15, DaFranzos/Pixabay; Page 17, GNNick/AdobeStock; Page 19, Worakit Sirijinda/AdobeStock; Page 21, kohy/AdobeStock; Page 23; electra kay-smith/AdobeStock; Page 25, picattos/AdobeStock; Page 27, GNNick/AdobeStock; Page 29, Denis Zaporozhtsev/AdobeStock; Page 31, monika porth/AdobeStock; Page 33, Dani/AdobeStock

Table of Contents

What Are Cassowaries?

Cassowaries are large birds. They are the third tallest bird in the world. Only ostriches and emus are taller.

There are three different kinds of cassowaries. They differ in where they live, their size, and their coloration.

Size

Most cassowaries grow to be between five and seven feet tall. The dwarf cassowary is usually only three feet tall.

Cassowaries are heavy birds. They can weigh up to 125 pounds.

Southern cassowaries are the

tallest of the three species.

Physical Characteristics

Cassowaries have lots of black feathers that look like hair. Their feathers protect them from sharp thorns and keep them dry.

They also have a casque, which is like a helmet on their head. It is made of **keratin**.

Scientists aren't sure what the casque is used for. It may be for self defense.

Habitat

Cassowaries are found in rainforests. There are lots of trees and plants in rainforests. It is very warm and wet there.

Not much light gets into parts of the rainforest. It can get very dark. Cassowaries can be hard to find because of their dark feathers.

Range

Cassowaries are found in the rainforests of Australia and New Guinea.

They are also found on some of the small islands around New Guinea.

Diet

Cassowaries are **omnivores**, which means that they eat meat and plants.

Most of their diet is fruits that they find in the rainforest. They also eat snails, frogs, bird eggs, and insects.

They use their sharp claws and

beak to find fruit on the ground

and in low bushes.

Cassowaries help the rainforest by spreading fruit seeds through their waste. The seeds that they drop can grow into new plants.

Many plants would not be able to spread to other parts of the rainforest without cassowaries.

Cassowaries are a **keystone species**. They are important to the plants and animals in their habitat.

Communication

Cassowaries make a special sound to communicate. It is very loud and sounds like a boom.

Cassowaries are often heard before they are seen. They blend into the shadows of trees in the rainforest.

Movement

Cassowaries can run up to thirty miles per hour. They can only run at that speed for short distances.

Cassowaries have strong legs. They can jump over seven feet high.

Cassowaries are one of the few birds that cannot fly. They are too big and heavy.

Self Defense

Cassowaries can be very dangerous. They have sharp claws that they use to protect themselves from **predators**.

They have been known to jump at a predator feet first. They do this so that their sharp claws will hit the predator.

Cassowaries can be shy. They probably wouldn't attack unless something bothered them.

Cassowary Chicks

Cassowaries lay between three and five green eggs at a time. The father takes care of the eggs until they hatch.

Cassowary chicks have brown and tan feathers when they hatch.

Chicks stay with their father

until they are about nine or ten

months old.

23

Solitary Life

Cassowaries are **solitary** birds. This means that they spend most of their time alone.

The only time they are seen together is when fathers are taking care of their chicks.

Cassowaries live deep in the rainforest. They are rarely seen by humans in the wild.

Lifespan

Not much is known about how long cassowaries live in the wild. This is because they are hard to find and study.

In **captivity**, they usually live between twenty and forty years. The oldest cassowary on record lived for 61 years.

Population

The Southern cassowary of Australia is **endangered**. There are not many left in the wild.

The populations of Northern and dwarf cassowaries are not known. They are hard to find and count in their rainforest habitat.

Cassowaries face threats like

habitat loss, being hit by cars,

and disease.

Helping Cassowaries

Cassowaries are in danger of being hit by cars when they cross the street.

Signs are placed along roads where cassowaries are known to be. They warn drivers to watch for cassowaries crossing the street.

CROSSING

The Cassowary Recovery Team is working to **preserve** cassowary habitats. They take care of rainforest land by planting trees.

They want to help Southern cassowaries by making sure they have a safe habitat to live in.

Glossary

Captivity: when animals are kept by people, not in the wild

Endangered: at risk of becoming extinct

Keratin: the protein that makes up human nails and hair

Keystone Species: a species that other animals in the ecosystem depend on

Omnivore: an animal that eats meat and plants

Predator: an animal that hunts other animals for food

Preserve: to keep safe

Solitary: living alone

About the Author

Victoria Blakemore is a first grade teacher in Southwest Florida with a passion for reading.

You can visit her at

www.elementaryexplorers.com

Also in This Series

Gray Wolves	Sloths	Flamingos	Camels	Koalas	Honey Bees	Pandas
Pangolins	White-Tailed Deer	Orcas	Giraffes	Corn	Meerkats	Echidnas
Walruses	Raccoons	Bald Eagles	Apples	Arctic Foxes	Red Pandas	Cassowaries
Tigers	Ladybugs	Moose	Beluga Whales	Leopards	Elephants	Jellyfish
Binturongs	Lions	Dolphins	Reindeer	Hammerhead Sharks	Hippos	Pumpkins
Peafowl	Chameleons	Florida Panthers	Aye-Ayes	Black Bears	Cheetahs	Manatees
Gingerbread	Polar Bears	Hot Chocolate	Orangutans	Coyotes	Marshmallows	Strawberries

All titles by Victoria Blakemore — Elementary Explorers

Also in This Series

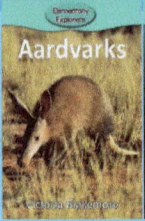

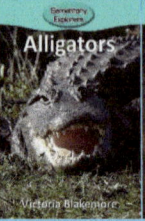

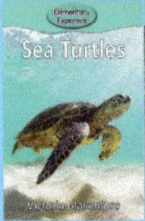

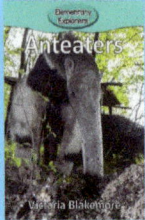

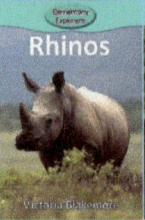

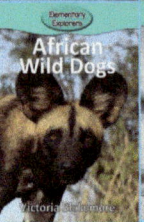

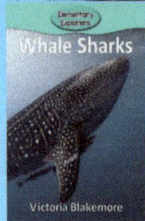

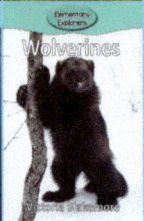

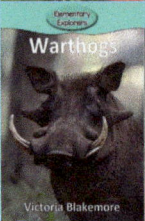

Aardvarks	Mako Sharks	Alligators	Frogs	Hedgehogs	Brown Bears	Bongos
Sea Turtles	Quokkas	Muskrats	Zebras	Red Foxes	Ring-Tailed Lemurs	Platypuses
Anteaters	Kangaroos	Rhinos	Jaguars	Wombats	Capybaras	Gorillas
Cats	Skunks	Butterflies	Dingoes	Snow Leopards	African Wild Dogs	Penguins
Whale Sharks	Wolverines	Warthogs	Caracals	Badgers	Seals	Hummingbirds

Victoria Blakemore